ORGANIC COOKBOOK

EMMA PATMORE

First published in 2000
for Tesco Stores Limited
by Brilliant Books Ltd
84-86 Regent Street
London W1B 5RR

ISBN 1-84221-134-X
Text and photographs © 2000 Brilliant Books Ltd

Origination by Colourpath Ltd, London
Printed and bound by Arti Grafiche Amilcare Pizzi, Italy

10 9 8 7 6 5 4 3 2 1

PICTURE CREDITS

Daniel Paingbourne: 102 (t). Images Colour Library: 2.
Mother and Baby Picture Library: 106. Soil Association: 6,
8 (l, t, cr). Telegraph Colour Library: 101. Tesco Recipe
Magazine: 98 (cr), 102 (b). Tony Stone Images: 8 (br),
98 (tl, cl), 102 (c). Trevor Vaughan: 98 (b). Ulla Nyeman: 104.
(Abbreviations: b=bottom, c=centre, l=left, r=right, t=top.)

ORGANIC COOKBOOK

EMMA PATMORE

ABOUT THE AUTHOR

Emma Patmore is a regular contributor to many national cookery magazines and has written several cookbooks. She really loves creating simple recipes that make the most of natural flavours. Her firm belief is that organic ingredients are not just healthier, but that they taste so much better, too.

Photographer   David Munns
Home economist   Emma Patmore
Stylist   Sam Scott
Recipes tested by Terry Farris

CONTENTS

NATURALLY DELICIOUS

This book is bursting with fresh ideas on how to maximise the flavour, texture and colour of the best natural ingredients. The dishes range from starters and snacks to sumptuous desserts, and there's even a special section for babies and toddlers. All the ingredients are organic and all the recipes are easy-to-follow and provide useful nutritional information, too. If you want to eat well and care about where your food comes from, The Organic Cookbook is for you!

USING THE RECIPES

The recipes in this book have been created and photographed for Tesco. They have been thoroughly tested and all ingredients used are organic, except for the seasonings. By its very nature, supply of organic produce is highly seasonal and subject to strict controls under which it can be grown. Therefore not all the ingredients may be available all the time from Tesco stores. However, as demand increases, the range of organic produce will become greater and greater. Fish, for example, will hopefully start to be available in 2001. 'Organic' is a legal definition. All products must be certified by a government approved body, registered with the UK Register of Organic Food Standards (UKROFS). All organic products stocked by Tesco are certified by the Soil Association or other UKROFS approved bodies.

Using the recipes: 1. Both metric and imperial weights and measures are given, except for goods sold in standard size packaging, such as cans. As conversions cannot always be exact, you should follow either the metric or the imperial throughout the recipe where possible. **2.** British standard level spoon measurements are used. A tablespoon measure is equivalent to 15ml; a teaspoon measure is equivalent to 5ml. **3.** Dishes cooked in the oven should be placed in the centre, unless otherwise stated. Tesco advises that all meat, poultry, fish and eggs should be cooked thoroughly. When cooked, poultry juices should run clear when the flesh is pierced with a skewer at its thickest point. **4.** Recipes containing soft ripened cheeses, sesame products, nuts or nut derivatives should not be eaten by children, people who have an allergic reaction to nuts, or women who are pregnant or breastfeeding. **5.** Vegetables and fruits used are medium-sized, unless otherwise specified. **6.** The fat and calorie content of each recipe is given. These figures are for one serving only. **7.** Each recipe has been given a simplicity rating of one, two or three chef's hats. One chef's hat means easy; two or three will require a little more effort.

CARROT AND LENTIL SOUP

Serves 4

Preparation 35 mins

Cooking time 35 mins

Calories 213

Fat 9g

Simplicity

1 Melt the butter with the oil in a saucepan and fry the carrots, onion and celery for 6–8 minutes or until lightly golden. Add the lentils and 750ml (1¼ pints) of vegetable stock and bring to the boil. Cover and simmer for about 20 minutes, until the carrots are tender.

2 Allow the soup to cool for about 15 minutes, then purée in a liquidiser or food processor, until smooth. Return to a clean saucepan with the remaining stock, add seasoning to taste and reheat gently before serving. Add a swirl of yogurt and a sprinkling of chopped fresh parsley, to garnish.

25g (1oz) butter
1 tbsp sunflower oil
450g (1lb) carrots, chopped
1 onion, chopped
2 celery sticks, chopped
100g (3½ oz) red split lentils, rinsed
850ml (1½ pints) vegetable stock
Sea salt and freshly ground black pepper
Natural yogurt and chopped fresh parsley, to garnish

It is best to wash organic carrots rather than peel them, as many of the nutrients are in the skin. It's no

On a cold winter's night, serve this thick, wholesome soup

myth that eating carrots really can improve your eyesight as they are an excellent source of beta

with warm crusty bread, for a simple and delicious meal.

carotene, which is essential for night vision and also helps keep the immune system working efficiently.

PROVENCAL-STYLE SOUP WITH SPRING ONION PESTO

Simplicity

Serves 4–6

Preparation 20 mins

Cooking time 25 mins

Calories 307–205

Fat 22–14g

2 tbsp extra virgin olive oil

1 onion, chopped

1 medium potato, peeled and chopped

1 carrot, chopped

1 yellow pepper, deseeded and chopped

500ml (18fl oz) garlic and herb stock, made from 1½ stock cubes

2 celery sticks, chopped

2 courgettes, chopped

400g can chopped tomatoes

1 tbsp tomato purée

Sea salt and freshly ground black pepper

For the pesto

6 spring onions, roughly chopped, including green part

50g (2oz) Parmesan, grated

4 tbsp extra virgin olive oil

1 For the soup, heat the oil in a large heavy-based saucepan, then add the onion, potato, carrot and yellow pepper. Cook uncovered for 5 minutes over a medium heat, stirring occasionally, until the vegetables just start to brown.

2 Add the stock, celery and courgettes and bring to the boil. Cover and simmer for 10 minutes or until the vegetables are tender. Stir in the tomatoes, tomato purée and season generously. Simmer uncovered for 10 minutes.

3 Meanwhile, make the pesto: place the spring onions, Parmesan and oil in a food processor and whizz together to a fairly smooth paste. Ladle the soup into bowls and top with a spoonful of the pesto.

All the flavours of the Mediterranean are packed into this

This soup is full of nutrients from all the vegetables, and it tastes fabulous, too. Onions contain

wonderful, fresh-tasting soup. The pesto, spooned on top,

allicin, which research shows may help to reduce cholesterol levels in the blood.

melts into the soup and adds a delicious kick.

CREAM OF MUSHROOM SOUP WITH CRISPY ONIONS

Serves 4

Preparation 15 mins

Cooking time 30 mins

Calories 378

Fat 32g

Simplicity

1 Heat the butter and oil in a large saucepan and fry the spring onions and mushrooms over a medium to high heat for 5 minutes, until softened and most of the juices have been evaporated.

2 Add the potato, vegetable stock and seasoning and bring to the boil. Reduce the heat, cover and simmer for 20 minutes until the potatoes are tender. Allow to cool.

3 Meanwhile, prepare the onions, heat about 1cm (½in) oil in a frying pan. Coat the onions in the flour, add to the pan and cook for 5 minutes or until crisp and lightly golden. Drain on kitchen paper.

4 Purée the soup in a liquidiser or food processor and return to the saucepan, stir in the cream and lemon juice and gently reheat. Ladle the soup into bowls and top with the crispy onions. Sprinkle with chopped fresh parsley, to garnish.

25g (1oz) butter
1 tbsp extra virgin olive oil
4 spring onions, chopped
2 x 200g punnets mushrooms, chopped
1 medium potato, peeled and chopped
850ml (1½ pints) vegetable stock
Sea salt and freshly ground black pepper
4 tbsp extra thick cream
Juice of ½ lemon
Chopped fresh parsley, to garnish

For the onions

Sunflower oil, for frying
1 large onion, finely sliced into rings
1 tbsp plain white flour

Mushrooms contain potassium, which can help to regulate blood pressure, copper, which aids the

This is a real comfort soup. The crispy fried onions on top

body's absorbtion of iron, and phosphorus, which is needed for healthy teeth and bones. The Chinese

are a great contrast to the smoothness of the soup.

believe certain varieties can be aphrodisiacs, so you may want to include them in your diet more often!

VEGETABLE TOASTS WITH TOMATO DRESSING

Simplicity 👨‍🍳 👨‍🍳

Serves 4

Preparation 20 mins

Cooking time 10 mins

Calories 284

Fat 15g

2 courgettes, thinly sliced lengthways

2 carrots, thinly sliced lengthways

2 red peppers, deseeded and thinly sliced

Sea salt and freshly ground black pepper

4 thick slices stonebaked white loaf

1 tbsp sunflower oil

For the dressing

2 tomatoes

4 tbsp extra virgin olive oil

2 spring onions, sliced

1 tbsp white wine vinegar

1 Place the courgettes, carrots and red peppers in a bowl and season well. (If you like you can use a vegetable peeler to make long ribbons with the courgettes and carrots.)

2 Toast the bread for 3 minutes each side or until golden brown. Meanwhile, for the dressing, place the tomatoes, in a bowl of boiling water for 30 seconds, then peel, deseed and finely chop.

3 Heat the sunflower oil in a large frying pan over a high heat, cook the vegetables for 4 minutes, stirring all the time, until they have softened and are just tender. Remove and set aside.

4 In the same pan, heat the olive oil and add the spring onions and white wine vinegar. Cook, stirring occasionally, for 1–2 minutes, until hot, then stir in the tomatoes. Pile the vegetables on top of the toasts, drizzle with the hot dressing and serve.

The dressing, drizzled over the pan-fried vegetables,

Beta carotene is the antioxidant and pigment found in many great-tasting brightly coloured vegetables.

soaks into the crispy toast, making a stunning dinner

Tomatoes get their colour from a different but particularly potent antioxidant pigment called lycopene.

party starter. Smaller versions make fabulous canapés.

VEGETABLE TEMPURA

Serves 4

Calories 355

Simplicity

Preparation 15 mins

Fat 16g

Cooking time 20 mins

1 To make the batter, lightly whisk together the eggs and water, then pour on to the flour all at once and whisk quickly, until the batter is smooth.

2 Heat the Cranberry and orange sauce in a small saucepan, over a gentle heat, until warm and runny. Remove from the heat and place in a bowl.

3 Heat 5cm (2in) of oil in a wok or frying pan. Dip the vegetables in to the batter and coat well. Test the temperature of the oil by dropping in a little batter, if it floats straight back to the surface the oil is hot enough.

4 Deep-fry the vegetables in small batches for 3–4 minutes or until crisp and golden. Remove with a slotted spoon and drain on kitchen paper. Season with salt. If using, deep-fry a few basil leaves for 20 seconds, until crisp. Serve the vegetables at once with the dipping sauce.

2 eggs
125ml (4fl oz) ice-cold water
70g (2½oz) plain white flour, sieved
225g jar Cranberry and orange sauce, for dipping
Vegetable oil, for deep-frying
1 courgette, cut into thick slices
1 large red onion, cut into wedges
225g (8oz) broccoli, cut into small florets
1 red pepper, deseeded and cut into strips
125g (4oz) green beans, topped only (not tailed)
125g (4oz) asparagus, trimmed
Sea salt
Fresh basil leaves, to garnish (optional)

Serve these vegetables, coated in a crispy, light batter, as

The way that tempura are cooked – quickly and at a high temperature – guarantees that very little

soon as possible after they have been cooked. Dunk them

of the water-soluble vitamins in the vegetables (such as B and C) are lost.

in the sweet dipping sauce and open wide...

ROOT VEGETABLE ROSTI

Simplicity

Serves 4
Preparation 25 mins
Cooking time 40 mins

Calories 293
Fat 16g

| 2 potatoes, peeled and coarsely grated |
| 1 parsnip, coarsely grated |
| 1 carrot, coarsely grated |
| 225g (8 oz) swede, coarsely grated |
| 15g (½ oz) butter, plus extra for greasing |
| 1 tbsp sunflower oil |
| 1 onion, chopped |
| 2.5cm (1 in) piece fresh root ginger, peeled and finely grated |
| 1 medium egg, beaten |
| 1 tbsp plain white flour |
| Sea salt and freshly ground black pepper |
| Crispy bacon, to serve (optional) |
| Fresh parsley, to garnish |

1 Preheat the oven to 190°C/375°F/Gas Mark 5. Place the grated potato, parsnip, carrot and swede in a clean tea towel and then squeeze out any excess liquid. Heat the butter and oil in a non-stick frying pan. Fry the onion and ginger for 5 minutes or until the onion has softened.

2 Place the grated vegetables in a large bowl, stir in the onion and ginger with the egg, flour and plenty of seasoning. Mound the mixture on to a greased baking sheet, to make a 20cm (8in) round. Bake for 30–35 minutes, until golden and crispy at the edges, and cooked through.

3 Carefully slide the vegetable rösti on to a large serving plate. Add the bacon (if using), garnish with fresh parsley and serve.

Rösti is Switzerland's answer to a plate of chips. This

The British get more vitamin C from potatoes than from any other food, and they aren't that high in calories.

version uses other root vegetables as well as traditional

To maximise their nutrients and their flavour, you could just scrub the potatoes instead of peeling them.

potatoes. Serve with a side salad, if liked.

GRILLED BRIE WITH BEETROOT SALAD

Serves 4

Preparation 15 mins

Cooking time 12 mins

Calories 403

Fat 25g

Simplicity

1 Peel and slice the avocado and place in a bowl together with the beetroot, celery and apple. Cover and set aside. Preheat the grill to high and lightly toast the bread for 2–3 minutes each side. Place a slice of Brie on top of each toast, then return them to the grill. Cook until the cheese is melted and slightly golden.

2 Meanwhile, to make the dressing, place all the ingredients in a small saucepan and bring to the boil, simmer for 2–3 minutes, until warmed through.

3 To serve, divide the salad leaves between four plates, top with the beetroot mixture and place a cheese toast on each plate. Drizzle over the warm dressing and serve immediately.

1 avocado

250g pack cooked beetroot, drained and chopped

2 celery sticks, sliced

1 red dessert apple, cored and chopped

4 slices stonebaked white loaf

1 portion Dutch Brie, approx. 125g (4oz), quartered

120g pack Alfresco salad

For the dressing

3 tbsp extra virgin olive oil

3 tbsp Cyder vinegar

1 garlic clove, crushed

1 small red onion, finely chopped

1 tbsp tomato purée

Sea salt and freshly ground black pepper

Creamy melted Brie, crusty bread, crisp and crunchy

Beetroot is high in folate, a nutrient which is linked to preventing anaemia and can relieve depression in

apples and celery, and sweet, soft beetroot make

the elderly. Beetroot is also one of the few vegetables that retains its nutrient content after boiling.

a wonderful contrast of flavours and textures.

CHICKEN AND ORANGE SALAD

Simplicity

Serves 4

Preparation 25 mins

Calories 240

Fat 10g

2 oranges

2 chicken breast fillets, cooked and shredded

2 celery sticks, cut into fine strips

2 spring onions, finely shredded

1 yellow pepper, deseeded and cut into fine strips

Sea salt and freshly ground black pepper

2 x 120g packs Alfresco salad

For the dressing

150ml (¼ pint) natural yogurt

2 tbsp mayonnaise

2 tsp clear honey

1 tbsp roughly chopped fresh parsley

1 Using a small, sharp knife, peel the oranges, working over a small bowl to reserve the juice. Cut away the flesh into segments and place in a separate bowl.

2 Stir in the cooked, shredded chicken, celery, spring onions and yellow pepper, and season well. Meanwhile, make the dressing: mix all the ingredients together, including the reserved orange juice, in a small bowl until well combined.

3 Arrange the salad leaves and chicken mixture between four plates and pour over the dressing.

If you fancy a change from chicken, try a smoked fish

Yogurt provides several useful nutrients, such as calcium and vitamin B2. The bacteria in live yogurt can

instead, such as mackerel. You can vary the dressing,

also help to keep the gut healthy and speed up the replacement of antibodies after a course of antibiotics.

too, by adding other herbs or a dollop of mustard.

BULGUR WHEAT SALAD WITH GRILLED PEPPERS

Serves 4

Preparation 35 mins

(including soaking time)

Cooking time 25 mins

Calories 480

Fat 26g

Simplicity

1 Place the bulgur wheat in a bowl and pour over boiling water to about 2cm (½in) above the level of the bulgur wheat and leave to soak for 20 minutes. Meanwhile, preheat the grill to high. Grill the yellow peppers, skin-side up, for 15–20 minutes, until the skin is blistered and blackened all over. Transfer to a plastic bag, seal and leave to cool. When cold enough to handle, remove and discard the charred skins and roughly chop the flesh.

2 Blanch the green beans in boiling water for 3–4 minutes, drain, refresh under cold running water and set aside. Put the tomatoes into a bowl, cover with boiling water and leave for 30 seconds. Peel, deseed, then roughly chop the flesh.

3 Combine the ingredients for the dressing and mix well. Drain the bulgur wheat and transfer to a salad bowl. Add the dressing and toss well. Add the vegetables, spring onions, brazil nuts, parsley and seasoning and toss together gently to mix.

225g (8oz) bulgur wheat

2 yellow peppers, quartered and deseeded

250g pack green beans, halved

2 ripe tomatoes

4 spring onions, sliced

75g (3oz) brazil nuts, roughly chopped

4 tbsp chopped fresh parsley

Sea salt and freshly ground black pepper

For the dressing

4 tbsp extra virgin olive oil

1 tbsp wholegrain mustard

1 garlic clove, crushed

1 tsp balsamic vinegar

1 tsp white wine vinegar

This salad is delicious, filling and extremely nutritious.

Combining a wide range of grains, nuts and vegetables is a good way for both vegetarians and vegans

The mustard and balsamic vinegar in the dressing bring

to stock up on the specific minerals they may be lacking, such as calcium, iron and zinc.

all the other exciting flavours of the salad alive.

ROASTED VEGETABLE SALAD

Simplicity

Serves 4

Preparation 15 mins

Cooking time 35 mins

Calories 340

Fat 15g

3 red onions, quartered

3 potatoes, scrubbed and cut into wedges

2 courgettes, thickly sliced

2 yellow peppers, deseeded and thickly sliced

4 tomatoes, halved

2 tbsp olive oil

Sea salt and freshly ground black pepper

Parmesan shavings (optional)

For the dressing

3 tbsp extra virgin olive oil

2 tbsp clear honey

1 tbsp balsamic vinegar

Finely grated rind and juice of ½ lemon

1 Preheat the oven to 200°C/400°F/Gas Mark 6. Place all the vegetables in a shallow roasting tin, drizzle over the olive oil and season. Shake the tray gently to ensure the vegetables are well coated with the oil and seasoning. Bake for about 35 minutes, until the vegetables are really tender and slightly charred at the edges.

2 Meanwhile, mix all the dressing ingredients together and pour this over the roasted vegetables, toss well and divide on to four plates, top with the Parmesan shavings, if using.

Roasting vegetables brings out their flavour and really

This salad combines a healthy mix of the antioxidant vitamins A, C and E, plus bags of minerals from the great-tasting

intensifies their natural sweetness. Serve with plenty of

vegetables. Remember, the more brightly-coloured the vegetables are, the more nutrients they are likely to contain.

fresh, crusty bread to soak up the yummy dressing.

VEGETABLE FRITTATA

Serves 4

Preparation 15 mins

Cooking time 30 mins

Calories 331

Fat 24g

Simplicity

1 Cook the asparagus and beans in a saucepan of boiling water for 5 minutes, add the peas, bring back to the boil, then immediately remove from the heat and drain well.

2 Melt the butter and oil in a large, heavy-based frying pan, 25.5cm (10in) wide and at least 1cm (½in) deep, with a heatproof handle. Fry the onions for 10 minutes until golden. Stir in the vegetables.

3 Meanwhile, preheat the grill to medium. Lightly beat the eggs with the parsley and seasoning. Pour the mixture into the pan and cook over a low heat for 10 minutes or until the base is set and golden.

4 Sprinkle the Parmesan, if using, over the frittata and place the frying pan under the grill. Cook for 3–4 minutes, until the top is golden brown and the frittata is cooked through. Serve fresh from the grill.

250g bunch asparagus, trimmed and cut into small pieces

150g (5oz) green beans, cut into small pieces

150g (5oz) frozen peas

25g (1oz) butter

2 tbsp extra virgin olive oil

2 onions, finely sliced

6 medium eggs

2 tbsp chopped fresh parsley

Sea salt and freshly ground black pepper

25g (1oz) freshly grated Parmesan (optional)

You can use almost anything you like in this omelette, but

Organic eggs have a wonderful flavour and a rich, thick yellowy yolk, which is a good source of iron.

avoid courgettes or other watery vegetables, as they can

The vegetables in this recipe provide plenty of vitamin C which the body needs to absorb iron efficiently.

stop the eggs from setting. Serve with a herby salad.

PASTA WITH DOUBLE TOMATO SAUCE

Simplicity

Serves 4

Preparation 10 mins

Cooking time 25 mins

Calories 385

Fat 13g

1 tbsp extra virgin olive oil

1 red onion, finely chopped

2 celery sticks, finely chopped

400g can chopped tomatoes

1 tbsp tomato purée

300ml (½ pint) vegetable stock

250g punnet cherry tomatoes, halved

1 tsp golden sugar

Sea salt and freshly ground black pepper

350g (12oz) dried pasta, such as gemelli or penne

4 tbsp crème fraîche (optional)

1 Heat the oil in a large, heavy-based saucepan, then add the red onion and celery and cook uncovered for 5 minutes over a medium heat, until the vegetables are tender. Add the chopped tomatoes, tomato purée and stock and bring to the boil. Simmer, uncovered, for 15 minutes, stirring occasionally, until reduced and thickened.

2 Add the cherry tomatoes, the sugar and season generously, then stir gently for about 3 minutes, until heated through.

3 Meanwhile, cook the pasta according to packet instructions, until al dente, then drain. Pour the sauce over the pasta, toss gently to avoid breaking the cherry tomatoes and serve with a dollop of crème fraîche, if using.

The cherry tomatoes added at the end of cooking keep

Research suggests that regular consumption of tomatoes, as part of a balanced diet, can lower the risk of

their shape and cut through the richness of the cooked

prostate cancer. This is due to something called lycopene – the pigment which gives tomatoes their colour.

tomato sauce. Serve with a green salad.

VEGETABLE STIR-FRY WITH NOODLES

Serves 4
Preparation 25 mins
Cooking time 15 mins

Calories 474
Fat 22g

Simplicity

1 Cook the noodles according to the packet instructions, then drain well. Meanwhile, make the sauce: mix together the peanut butter, tomato purée, balsamic vinegar and seasoning, with about 4 tablespoons of cold water. Set aside.

2 Heat the oil in a wok or large frying pan until very hot. Add the garlic, carrots and green beans and stir-fry for 2 minutes, until lightly coloured. Add the broccoli and stir-fry for 2–3 minutes or until softened. Add the red pepper and spring onions, then cook for a further 1 minute.

3 Add the sauce, 125ml (4fl oz) water and the drained noodles. Combine well and stir-fry for 4–5 minutes or until everything is hot. Garnish with chopped fresh coriander and serve with fresh lemon wedges to squeeze over.

* Those with an allergy to nuts, children under five and pregnant women should avoid all nuts.

250g pack broad ribbon egg noodles

2 tbsp sunflower oil

1 garlic clove, sliced

2 carrots, thinly sliced diagonally

150g (5oz) green beans, halved

150g (5oz) broccoli florets

1 red pepper, deseeded and cut into matchsticks

4 spring onions, thinly sliced diagonally

For the sauce

4 tbsp smooth peanut butter*

1 tbsp tomato purée

1 tbsp balsamic vinegar

Sea salt and freshly ground black pepper

Chopped fresh coriander, to garnish

Lemon wedges, to serve

This stir-fry has a secret ingredient – the peanut butter

Like most other nuts, peanuts are high in 'healthy' monounsaturated fats and low in 'unhealthy'

adds instant sweetness and depth of flavour. You can use

saturated fats. They are also an extremely useful source of both vitamin E and zinc.

whatever vegetables you happen to have in the fridge.

TOMATO RICE

Simplicity

Serves 4

Preparation 10 mins

Cooking time 25 mins

Calories 356

Fat 10g

2 tbsp extra virgin olive oil, plus extra to serve (optional)
1 large onion, finely chopped
225g (8oz) white fragrant rice
2 x 400g cans chopped tomatoes
450ml (¾ pint) vegetable stock
Sea salt and freshly ground black pepper
40g (1½ oz) Parmesan, finely grated, plus extra to serve (optional)
2 spring onions, finely sliced

1 Heat the oil in a large, heavy-based saucepan, then fry the onion for 5 minutes until soft and lightly golden. Add the rice, stirring well to coat all the grains with oil and cook for 1 minute.

2 Add the tomatoes, vegetable stock and seasoning and bring to the boil. Reduce the heat, then cover and simmer for 10–15 minutes or until the rice is just cooked.

3 Stir through the Parmesan and the spring onions and cook for a further 2 minutes. Serve sprinkled with extra grated Parmesan and a generous drizzle of olive oil, if wished.

This is like a risotto, but you don't have to stir it the whole time. If you like garlic, add a couple of crushed cloves with the rice. Try serving it with a green salad.

The organic rice in this satisfying dish provides a convenient source of carbohydrates and therefore a steady supply of energy. The tomatoes provide plenty of vitamin C which helps wounds to heal quickly.

TOMATO, MUSTARD AND BRIE TART

Serves 4

Preparation 45 mins

(including chilling time)

Cooking time 50 mins

Calories 554

Fat 38g

Simplicity

1 Sift the flour and a pinch of sea salt into a bowl, rub the butter in, using your fingertips, until it resembles fine breadcrumbs. Add 2 tablespoons of cold water and mix to a dough. Cover and refrigerate for 20 minutes. Use the pastry to line a deep 20cm (8in) metal flan tin and chill for a further 10 minutes.

2 Preheat the oven to 190°C/375°F/Gas Mark 5. Line the pastry with baking paper and baking beans, then bake blind for 10–12 minutes. Carefully remove the paper and beans and bake the pastry for a further 5 minutes. Set aside, then reduce the oven temperature to 180°C/350°F/Gas Mark 4.

3 In a jug, beat together the milk, egg yolks, garlic and seasoning. Spread the mustard over the base of the pastry and sprinkle over the Cheddar. Arrange the tomatoes and Brie on top and pour over the egg mixture. Cook for 30–35 minutes, until just set and golden. For the herb oil, mix all the ingredients together and drizzle over the tart. Serve warm.

175g (6oz) plain white flour

Sea salt and freshly ground black pepper

75g (3oz) butter, diced

125ml (4floz) milk

2 medium egg yolks

1 garlic clove, crushed

1 tbsp wholegrain mustard

50g (2oz) medium/mature Cheddar, grated

4 ripe tomatoes, sliced

1 portion Dutch Brie, approx. 125g (4oz), thinly sliced

For the herb oil

1 tbsp finely shredded fresh basil

1 tbsp finely chopped fresh parsley

1 tbsp finely chopped fresh coriander

2 tbsp extra virgin olive oil

This tart has a lovely combination of melting cheese, ripe

This tart is great on family picnics, full of energy-giving calories for children. The cheeses in this

tomatoes and crisp pastry. The herb oil that is drizzled

recipe are also a rich source of calcium which helps build and maintain strong bones.

over the top, accentuates the fabulous fresh flavours.

PASTA, CAULIFLOWER AND BROCCOLI BAKE

Simplicity 🧑‍🍳🧑‍🍳

Serves 4

Preparation 15 mins

Cooking time 40 mins

Calories 641

Fat 20g

275g (10oz) cauliflower, cut into small florets

225g (8oz) broccoli, cut into small florets

450ml (¾ pint) semi-skimmed milk

50g (2oz) butter

3 tbsp plain white flour, sieved

200g (7oz) mature Cheddar, grated

1 tbsp wholegrain mustard

Sea salt and freshly ground black pepper

375g (13oz) dried pasta, such as penne

For the topping

50g (2oz) fresh breadcrumbs, made from 2 slices stonebaked white loaf, crusts removed

2 spring onions, finely chopped

25g (1oz) butter, melted

1 Preheat the oven to 200°C/400°F/Gas Mark 6. Add the cauliflower to a saucepan of boiling water, then simmer, covered for 4 minutes. Add the broccoli to the pan, cover and simmer for a further 2 minutes, then drain well.

2 Meanwhile, make the sauce: place the milk, butter and flour in a large saucepan and gently heat. Bring slowly to the boil, whisking with a wire whisk, until the mixture thickens. Cook for a further 2 minutes, stirring all the time. Mix in 175g (6oz) of the Cheddar, the mustard and seasoning, remove from the heat and stir until the cheese has melted.

3 Cook the pasta according to packet instructions, until al dente, drain and gently mix with the vegetables. Add the cheese sauce to the pasta, mix well, then transfer to an ovenproof dish. Mix all the topping ingredients together with the remaining Cheddar and sprinkle over the pasta. Bake for 15–20 minutes or until golden and bubbling.

This satisfying pasta bake, with its cheese sauce and

Like all cruciferous vegetables, including cabbage and Brussels sprouts, cauliflower and broccoli contain

crunchy golden topping, is a great way to get your

important natural chemicals called isothiocyanates, which may offer some protection against cancer.

children to eat vegetables. Grown-ups will love it, too...

GOAT'S CHEESE SOUFFLES WITH BEETROOT SALAD

Serves 4

Preparation 25 mins

Cooking time 25 mins

Calories 383

Fat 28g

Simplicity

1 Grease four 125ml (4fl oz) ramekins with the melted butter. Preheat the oven to 190°C/375°F/Gas Mark 5. Melt the remaining butter in a saucepan, stir in the flour and cook over a low heat for 1 minute, stirring. Remove from the heat and gradually add the milk, stirring, to keep the mixture smooth. Simmer over a low heat for 4–5 minutes, stirring frequently. Remove from the heat, stir in the mustard, seasoning, egg yolks, goat's cheese and spring onions.

2 In a large bowl, whisk the egg whites with a pinch of salt to form soft-peaks. Gently fold a quarter of the egg whites into the cheese mixture, then fold this into the remaining egg whites. Spoon into the ramekins and sprinkle with the Parmesan.

3 Place on a baking sheet and bake the soufflés for 15–20 minutes, until well risen and golden. Meanwhile, mix all the salad ingredients together and season. Remove the soufflés from the ramekins and serve with the salad leaves and beetroot salad.

35g (1¼ oz) butter (plus 1 tbsp melted butter, for greasing)

25g (1oz) plain white flour

225ml (8fl oz) whole milk

1 tsp wholegrain mustard

Sea salt and freshly ground black pepper

2 medium eggs, separated

100g pack Welsh goat's cheese

2 spring onions, finely chopped

2 tbsp freshly grated Parmesan

120g pack Alfresco salad

For the salad

250g pack cooked beetroot, drained and finely chopped

1 red onion, finely chopped

2 tbsp chopped fresh parsley

2 tbsp olive oil

1 tbsp red wine vinegar

If you want to serve these soufflés at a dinner party, they

Because there is no vitamin B12 in either vegetables or fruit, vegetarians tend to get much of their supply

can be prepared an hour in advance, up to the end of

from cheese and eggs. This recipe is particularly rich in vitamin B12 – an essential nutrient for growth.

step 2. You can then bake them at the last minute.

GREEN VEGETABLE PESTO PASTA

Simplicity

Serves 4

Preparation 15 mins

Cooking time 10 mins

Calories 457

Fat 20g

275g (10oz) dried pasta, such as gemelli

150g (5oz) green beans, halved

125g (4oz) broccoli, cut into small florets

1 courgette, cut into matchsticks

For the pesto

15g pack fresh basil, plus extra leaves, to garnish (optional)

1 garlic clove, crushed

50g (2oz) Parmesan, grated

25g (1oz) cashew nuts

4 tbsp extra virgin olive oil

Sea salt and freshly ground black pepper

1 To make the pesto, place the basil, garlic, Parmesan, cashew nuts and olive oil in a food processor and pulse until smooth. Season to taste and set aside.

2 Meanwhile, bring a saucepan of salted water to the boil. Add the pasta and cook for 6 minutes. Add the beans and cook for 1 minute, then add the rest of the vegetables and cook for a further 2 minutes. Drain thoroughly.

3 Return the pasta and vegetables to the saucepan and stir in the pesto. Heat gently for about 1 minute, until well combined and hot. Serve garnished with extra basil, if wished.

Traditionally, pesto is made with pine nuts, but you can

The vegetables in this dish provide fibre, minerals and vitamins, especially broccoli which is an excellent

make it with other nuts, too. Why not give brazil nuts,

source of vitamin C. The darker the florets, the more health-giving nutrients the broccoli is likely to contain.

pistachios or cashew nuts a try for a change?

BUBBLE AND SQUEAK WITH RED ONION CHUTNEY

Serves 4

Preparation 25 mins

Cooking time 30 mins

Calories 302

Fat 9g

Simplicity ♟ ♟

1 Place the potatoes and garlic in a saucepan and cover with water. Bring to the boil, cover and simmer for 15–20 minutes, until tender. Drain, return to the pan and mash until smooth. Cool.

2 Meanwhile, place the cabbage in a saucepan and pour over boiling water to just cover, bring back to the boil, then drain. Add the cabbage, spring onions and seasoning to the potato and mix well.

3 Place all the ingredients for the chutney in a saucepan and bring to the boil over a low heat. Simmer gently, uncovered, for about 20 minutes or until almost all of the liquid has evaporated.

4 Divide the potato into eight and shape into flat rounds. Melt the butter and oil in a frying pan and fry the cakes for 5 minutes on one side over a medium heat. Turn over, taking care as the cakes are quite soft, and cook for a further 5 minutes, until golden and heated through. Serve with the chutney.

675g (1lb 8oz) potatoes, peeled and cut into even-sized pieces
1 garlic clove, peeled
125g (4oz) Savoy cabbage, finely shredded
4 spring onions, finely sliced
Sea salt and freshly ground black pepper
25g (1oz) butter
1 tbsp sunflower oil

For the onion chutney

2 large red onions, or 6 small red onions, finely chopped
50g (2oz) golden sugar
1 tbsp white wine vinegar

Originally a recipe to use up the leftovers from the Sunday

Eating cabbage twice a week, as part of a balanced diet, may help to ward off cancer of the colon.

roast, bubble and squeak is now found on the smartest

To stop cabbage smelling and preserve its vitamin C, boil it uncovered and don't cook it for too long.

restaurant menus. It's wonderful with the sweet chutney.

COURGETTE AND CHEESE GRATIN

Simplicity

Serves 4

Preparation 10 mins

Cooking time 30 mins

Calories 257

Fat 18g

---

4 large courgettes, sliced diagonally

400g can chopped tomatoes

2 tbsp shredded fresh basil

Sea salt and freshly ground black pepper

2 x 125g packs Italian mozzarella, drained and sliced

15g (½ oz) freshly grated Parmesan

1 tbsp extra virgin olive oil

---

1 Preheat the oven to 200°C/400°F/Gas mark 6. Blanch the courgettes in boiling water for about 4 minutes, drain well and then thoroughly dry them using kitchen paper.

2 Drain the canned tomatoes in a sieve to remove all excess liquid. Layer half the courgettes in a shallow, ovenproof dish, spread with half the sieved tomatoes, then sprinkle with half the basil and a little seasoning. Place half of the mozzarella slices on top in an even layer.

3 Repeat the layers once again, sprinkle with Parmesan, drizzle with olive oil and then cook for about 25 minutes or until golden, bubbling and tender. Serve as a main course, with some garlic bread, or it would be a lovely accompaniment to most chicken dishes.

Everyone will love this quick, easy and filling dish. Allow

Courgettes contain carotenes, folate and vitamin C, which are all essential for a healthy immune system.

it to stand for 5 minutes after it comes out of the oven, to

They also provide useful amounts of potassium which helps the body to maintain normal blood pressure.

let the flavours infuse. Try serving it with new potatoes.

PASTA WITH GOAT'S CHEESE AND ASPARAGUS

Serves 4 **Calories** 568 **Simplicity**

Preparation 10 mins **Fat** 26g

Cooking time 20 mins

1 Heat the oil and butter in a frying pan, cook the onion over a medium heat for 7 minutes, stirring occasionally. Add the garlic and cook for a further 3 minutes, until the onions are golden and crisp.

2 Meanwhile, bring a large saucepan of salted water to the boil. Add the pasta and cook for 5 minutes, add the asparagus and cook for a further 2 minutes, then add the peas and cook for 2 minutes. When cooked, drain well.

3 Return the pasta and vegetables to the saucepan and gently stir through nearly all of the onions, saving a small amount for garnish. Add the goat's cheese and plenty of freshly ground black pepper and mix together well. Serve topped with the remaining crispy onions.

1 tbsp sunflower oil
25g (1oz) butter
2 red onions, thinly sliced
1 garlic clove, finely chopped
Sea salt and freshly ground black pepper
275g (10oz) dried pasta, such as penne
250g bunch asparagus, trimmed and cut into small pieces
150g (5oz) peas, fresh or frozen
2 x 100g packs Welsh goat's cheese, roughly crumbled

The combination of crispy onions, melting goat's cheese and delicate asparagus spears go together beautifully in this fast and fashionable pasta dish.

Asparagus and peas are rich in folate and antioxidants. Asparagus is also a mild laxative and natural diuretic and can be used to relieve fluid retention. Herbalists also use it to soothe indigestion.

SALMON WITH ONION AND RED WINE BUTTER

Simplicity

Serves 4

Preparation 25 mins
(plus 1 hour chilling)

Cooking time 15 mins

Calories 507

Fat 37g

---

1 tbsp sunflower oil

4 salmon fillets,* weighing about
175g (6oz) each, skinned

For the butter

150ml (¼ pint) red wine

½ small red onion,
finely chopped

75g (3oz) butter, softened

2 tbsp finely chopped fresh
parsley, plus extra, to garnish

1 garlic clove, very
finely chopped

Sea salt and freshly ground
black pepper

Availability planned from 2001

1 To prepare the butter, place the wine and onion in a small saucepan and bring to the boil. Boil rapidly for about 4–5 minutes over a high heat or until reduced to about 2 tablespoons. Remove from the heat and allow to cool completely.

2 In a bowl, beat the butter until smooth, add the parsley, garlic, seasoning and reduced wine and mix together with a fork. Place the butter on a piece of greaseproof paper and roll up into a tight sausage shape. Place in the fridge and chill until hardened.

3 Wash and wipe the salmon with kitchen paper. Heat the oil in a large frying pan over a medium heat and cook the salmon for 4 minutes. Turn and cook for 3–4 minutes more, until cooked through.

4 Cut the butter into four pieces and place one on top of each salmon fillet. Allow the butter to melt by cooking for 2 minutes more before serving.

Flavoured butter is a great way to jazz up pan-fried fish

Oil-rich fish, such as salmon, may help lessen the extent of inflammation caused by diseases such as

or meat. It works so well, you may want to make up

arthritis. The oils have also been linked to the healthy development of a baby's brain during pregnancy.

more and keep the rest in the freezer for next time.

WARM SALMON SALAD

Serves 4   **Calories** 536   **Simplicity**

Preparation 30 mins   **Fat** 39g

Cooking time 15 mins

1 Cook the eggs in simmering water for about 7 minutes, add the green beans and cook for a further 3 minutes. Drain, and set the green beans aside; shell and quarter the eggs and set aside.

2 Meanwhile, wash, and wipe the fish fillets with kitchen paper, then place in a shallow frying pan. Just cover with water and bring to the boil, cover and simmer for 5 minutes. Remove from the heat and leave for 5 minutes or until cooked and beginning to flake. Drain the fish, skin, then flake into pieces.

3 For the dressing, combine all the ingredients together in a small bowl. Heat 5cm (2in) of oil in a frying pan, over a high heat, and fry the potatoes for 5–6 minutes, until golden and crisp. Drain on kitchen paper and season with salt. In a large bowl, combine the beans, eggs, flaked salmon, onion, cherry tomatoes and dressing. To serve, arrange the salad leaves on plates, place the salmon on top with the potatoes and garnish with basil leaves.

3 medium eggs
75g (3oz) green beans, chopped
3 salmon fillets*
Sunflower oil, for deep frying
225g (8oz) baby new potatoes, sliced very thinly
1 small red onion, finely sliced
125g (4oz) cherry tomatoes, halved
120g pack Alfresco salad
Fresh basil leaves, to garnish

For the dressing

4 tbsp olive oil
2 tsp red wine vinegar
2 tsp balsamic vinegar
1 garlic clove, crushed
Sea salt and freshly ground black pepper

Availability planned from 2001

This recipe is based on the classic Salade Niçoise, but it

Salmon contains valuable omega oils, which, if eaten regularly, as part of a balanced diet, are thought

uses fresh salmon, instead of tuna. It's great on its own, or

to reduce the risk of heart disease. Organic salmon has a firm flesh, great flavour and natural colour.

you can serve it with fresh, warm crusty bread.

SALMON WITH ASPARAGUS, BALSAMIC AND ORANGE

Simplicity

Serves 4

Preparation 10 mins

Cooking time 25 mins

Calories 385

Fat 25g

2 tbsp extra virgin olive oil

Finely grated rind of ½ orange, plus the juice of 1 orange

Sea salt and freshly ground black pepper

250g bunch asparagus, trimmed

4 salmon steaks,* weighing about 175g (6oz) each

1 tbsp balsamic vinegar

2 tbsp chopped fresh coriander

Availability planned for 2001

1 Pre-heat the oven to 200°C/400°F/Gas Mark 6. Place 1 tablespoon of the olive oil on a baking tray with the grated orange rind and seasoning. Add the asparagus and toss well in the oil mixture. Cook for 15–20 minutes or until tender.

2 Meanwhile, wash and wipe the salmon with kitchen paper and season. Heat the remaining oil in a large frying pan over a medium heat. Add the salmon to the pan and cook for 4–5 minutes each side or until golden and cooked right through.

3 Add the balsamic vinegar and orange juice and simmer for about 2 minutes until the sauce is bubbling and warmed through, stir in the coriander and serve straight away with the asparagus.

The fresh tangy citrus flavours and balsamic

The rind of organic citrus fruit can be used in cooking without worrying about the wax, which non-organic

vinegar cut through the richness of the salmon.

fruit is sometimes sprayed with to make it shiny. Oranges are an excellent source of vitamin C.

Delicious, served simply with new potatoes.

KEDGEREE WITH TROUT

Serves 4

Preparation 20 mins

Cooking time 25 mins

Calories 782

Fat 32g

Simplicity

1 Rinse the fish, place in a shallow saucepan and just cover with water. Bring to the boil, then simmer, covered, for 5 minutes. Remove from the heat and leave for 5 minutes. Drain and reserve the water. Add more water to make up to 600ml (1 pint), then crumble in the stock cube. Cook the eggs in simmering water for 10 minutes until hard-boiled.

2 In a large saucepan, heat the oil and sauté the onion, celery and lemon rind for 5 minutes over a medium heat, until softened. Stir in the rice and coat well. Add the stock to the rice mixture, cover and simmer for 12 minutes. Add the peas and continue to cook for a further 3 minutes, until the rice is just tender.

3 Meanwhile, skin and flake the trout, shell and quarter the eggs. Stir them into the rice with the butter, cream and seasoning, until the mixture is well combined and warmed through. Sprinkle with the parsley and serve with lemon wedges, if wished.

4 rainbow trout fillets,* weighing about 350g (12oz) each

1 vegetable stock cube

3 medium eggs

1 tbsp sunflower oil

1 onion, chopped

3 celery sticks, chopped

Finely grated rind of 1 lemon

200g (7oz) white fragrant rice

50g (2oz) frozen peas

25g (1oz) butter

2 tbsp extra thick cream or crème fraîche

Sea salt and freshly ground black pepper

4 tbsp finely chopped fresh parsley

Lemon wedges, to serve (optional)

Availability planned for 2001

Although a traditional breakfast dish, this tastes great

Rice supplies complex carbohydrates, which can help to stabilise blood sugar levels. Eating oil-rich fish

at lunchtime, suppertime or even at two in the morning!

twice a week during pregnancy may help the healthy development of a baby's eyes and brain.

The celery adds a delicious crunch to the buttery rice.

GRILLED TROUT WITH BLUE CHEESE AND APPLE

Simplicity

Serves 4

Preparation 15 mins

Cooking time 7 mins

Calories 603

Fat 33g

4 trout fillets,* skin left on

2 tsp olive oil, plus extra, for greasing

Freshly ground black pepper

75g (3oz) extra creamy Danish blue, crumbled

2 tbsp chopped fresh parsley

1 apple, cored and finely chopped

25g (1oz) almonds, chopped

Juice of 1 lemon

Availability planned for 2001

1 Pre-heat the grill to high. Wash and wipe the fish fillets with kitchen paper and place skin-side down on an oiled baking tray. Brush lightly with the oil and season with freshly ground black pepper. Grill the fish for 4 minutes.

2 Meanwhile, prepare the topping by mixing together the cheese, parsley, apple and almonds in a bowl. Remove the fish from the grill and divide the topping between the fillets. Return to the grill and cook for a further 2–3 minutes until the topping is golden and bubbling and the fish is cooked through. Sprinkle with the lemon juice and serve straight away.

Although it may sound like an unusual combination, the strong flavours of the trout and blue cheese work really well together. Serve with new potatoes and a salad.

An apple a day may not always keep the doctor away, but the pectin in cooked apples can help ease the effects of an upset stomach. A lot of an apple's vitamin C content is found in the skin.

ROAST CHICKEN WITH BASIL AND RED ONIONS

Serves 4

Preparation 20 mins

(plus 10 mins resting)

Cooking time 1 hr 10 mins

Calories 502

Fat 35g

Simplicity

1 Preheat the oven to 190°C/375°F/Gas Mark 5. Place the chicken in a roasting tray. Gently work the skin away from the flesh with your fingers and tuck about 6–7 basil leaves under the breast skin of the chicken. Place the remaining basil in a liquidiser with the olive oil, lemon juice and seasoning and whizz until smooth. Brush the chicken with half the basil oil and cook for 40 minutes.

2 Meanwhile, prepare the onions: peel them and then slice off the root bottom end to give a flat base. Make four cuts, in a criss-cross shape, across the top of each onion to come only halfway down, so that the onions open slightly. Combine the lemon rind with the garlic and sprinkle this over the onions.

3 Add the onions to the chicken in the tray and brush well with some of the basil oil. Brush the remaining oil over the chicken and cook for a further 40 minutes or until cooked through. Cover and allow the chicken to rest for 10 minutes before carving.

1 chicken, weighing about 1.4kg (3lb 2oz), metal tag on wing removed

15g pack fresh basil

6 tbsp extra virgin olive oil

Juice of ½ lemon

Sea salt and freshly ground black pepper

For the onions

4 medium red onions

Grated rind of ½ lemon

1 garlic clove, crushed

Tucking basil leaves under the skin adds great flavour and guarantees this simple roast chicken always goes down well. The red onions are the perfect accompaniment.

Chicken is a great source of low-fat protein as long as you don't eat the skin, which can almost treble its fat content. As part of a balanced diet, eating plenty of onions may help to reduce cholesterol levels.

OVEN-BAKED PARMESAN CHICKEN

Simplicity

Serves 4

Preparation 25 mins

Cooking time 20 mins

Calories 334

Fat 18g

25g (1oz) fresh breadcrumbs, made from 1 slice stonebaked white loaf, crusts removed

75g (3oz) Parmesan, finely grated

2 spring onions, finely chopped

Finely grated rind and juice of ½ lemon

50g (2oz) butter, melted

Sea salt and freshly ground black pepper

4 skinless chicken breast fillets

2 tbsp chopped fresh parsley

1 Preheat the oven to 190°C/375°F/Gas Mark 5. Mix the breadcrumbs, Parmesan, spring onions, lemon rind, butter and seasoning together in a small bowl. Divide the mixture between the chicken breasts and using a fork, press the mixture down on top, to form an even coat.

2 Transfer the chicken breasts to a shallow roasting tin and bake for 20 minutes. Remove the chicken from the roasting tin and keep warm. Add the lemon juice and parsley to the buttery juices in the tin and mix well. Pour these juices over the chicken and serve straight away.

Cooked in a coat of Parmesan and breadcrumbs, the

High-protein foods are an excellent choice for those who are convalescing, and chicken is no exception.

chicken breasts keep moist and succulent. Serve with

It is also a good source of zinc and vitamin A, both of which help to speed up the body's repair process.

new potatoes and a salad or a green vegetable.

CHICKEN KEBABS WITH COUSCOUS

Serves 4

Preparation 30 mins

(plus 1 hour marinating)

Cooking time 12 mins

Calories 499

Fat 14g

Simplicity

1 Place the chicken and peppers in a non-metallic bowl, add the lemon juice, garlic, olive oil and coriander and mix. Cover and leave to marinate for at least 1 hour. Meanwhile, combine all the ingredients for the sauce. Season and leave to chill. Soak four large wooden skewers in water for about 10 minutes.

2 Preheat the grill to high. Thread the chicken and peppers onto the skewers and grill for 10–12 minutes, turning occasionally, until the chicken is slightly charred and cooked through and tender. Keep warm.

3 Meanwhile, prepare the couscous according to packet instructions, then fluff up with a fork. Melt the butter in a small saucepan and fry the spring onions for about 2 minutes. Add the spring onions with 3 tablespoons of chopped coriander and plenty of seasoning to the couscous and mix well. Serve the couscous on plates, with the kebabs on top, then drizzle with the yogurt sauce.

4 chicken breast fillets, skin removed and cut into 24 pieces

1 yellow and 1 red pepper, deseeded and cut into 8 pieces

Juice of 1 lemon

2 garlic cloves, crushed

2 tbsp extra virgin olive oil

1 tbsp chopped fresh coriander

For the sauce

150ml (¼ pint) natural yogurt

1 tbsp lemon juice

Finely grated rind of ½ lemon

Sea salt and freshly ground black pepper

For the couscous

250g (9oz) couscous

25g (1oz) butter

4 spring onions, finely chopped

3 tbsp chopped fresh coriander

The lemony marinade infuses the chicken and peppers

Couscous, with its pleasant nutty taste, is easy to digest and helps keep blood sugars stable. Sweet

with its lovely flavour, but it also starts to tenderise the

peppers are an excellent source of vitamin C, needed for healthy teeth, gums, bones and skin.

meat. Leave to marinate overnight, if possible.

CHICKEN STIR-FRY WITH LEMON AND MANGO

Simplicity

Serves 4

Preparation 25 mins

Cooking time 10 mins

Calories 257

Fat 7g

1 ripe mango

2 tbsp sunflower oil

2 garlic cloves, crushed

2.5cm (1in) piece fresh root ginger, finely chopped

4 chicken breast fillets, cut into strips

150g (5oz) mangetout, halved lengthways

2 celery sticks, thinly sliced

1 yellow pepper, deseeded and cut into matchsticks

4 spring onions, thinly sliced

Sea salt and freshly ground black pepper

Juice of ½ lemon

2 tbsp white wine or apple juice

1 tbsp balsamic vinegar

1 tbsp clear honey

2 tbsp chopped fresh coriander

1 To prepare the mango, slice the two fatter 'cheeks' of the mango from either side of the stone. Cut a criss-cross pattern across the flesh of each piece to divide into small cubes, then push the skin upwards and slice off the cubes. Set aside.

2 Heat the oil in a wok or large frying pan until hot. Add the garlic and ginger with the chicken and stir-fry for 3 minutes.

3 Add the mangetout, celery and yellow pepper and stir-fry for 3–4 minutes. Add the spring onions, mango and seasoning, and then stir-fry for a further 2 minutes.

4 Combine the lemon juice with the white wine or apple juice, balsamic vinegar and honey in a small bowl. Add to the wok and continue to cook for a further 2 minutes. Add the coriander and serve.

The familiar pairing of lemon and chicken is given an

Both the mango and the mangetout in this stir-fry provide beta carotene. The mangetout are also a good

unusual, but wonderful lift by the perfumed mango.

source of vitamin C, but since the vitamin is water soluble, try to cook them for as short a time as possible.

Great served with egg noodles or rice on the side.

LAMB CASSEROLE WITH COUSCOUS AND GREMOLATA

Serves 4

Preparation 30 mins

Cooking time 1 hour

Calories 681

Fat 25g

Simplicity

1 Pre-heat the oven to 180°C/350°F/Gas Mark 4. Season the flour and place on a large plate, toss the meat until coated. Heat the oil in a large frying pan and cook the meat, over a medium heat, for 2–3 minutes each side, until browned (you will need to do this in two batches). Transfer the browned meat to a casserole dish, using a slotted spoon.

2 Add the peppers to the frying pan and cook for 2 minutes. Add the tomatoes and bring to the boil. Add these to the lamb and cook in the oven for 40 minutes or until the meat is tender. Meanwhile, mix all the ingredients for the gremolata together.

3 Prepare the couscous according to packet instructions, then fluff up with a fork. Heat the oil in a small frying pan and cook the onion over a medium heat for 10 minutes until golden brown. Add to the couscous and mix well. Sprinkle the gremolata over the lamb casserole and serve with the couscous.

Sea salt and freshly ground black pepper

2 tbsp plain white flour

2 x 400g packs diced lamb, trimmed of any excess fat

2–3 tbsp extra virgin olive oil

1 yellow and 1 green pepper, deseeded and chopped

400g can chopped tomatoes

For the gremolata

1 garlic clove, very finely chopped

3 tbsp finely chopped fresh parsley

Grated rind of 1 lemon

For the couscous

250g (9oz) couscous

1 tbsp extra virgin olive oil

1 large onion, finely sliced

Gremolata is a mixture of finely chopped herbs, garlic

Lamb is an excellent source of zinc – one of the vital minerals needed for a healthy immune system.

and citrus rind. Adding this to the casserole, just before

This casserole is also full of vitamin C from the lemon, peppers and tomatoes.

serving, lends a fresh new dimension of flavour.

LAMB CHOPS WITH CRANBERRY AND ORANGE

Simplicity

Serves 4
Preparation 20 mins
Cooking time 15 mins

Calories 465
Fat 22g

150ml (¼ pint) red wine

125ml (4fl oz) vegetable stock

225g jar Cranberry and orange sauce

15g (½ oz) butter, chilled

2 tsp oil, for frying

12 lamb chops, trimmed of excess fat

For the salsa

Grated rind (optional) and flesh of 1 orange

3 spring onions, finely sliced

3 tbsp chopped fresh parsley

1 tsp olive oil

1 Place the wine and stock in a small saucepan and bring to the boil. Boil rapidly for 5–6 minutes over a high heat or until reduced by half. Stir in the Cranberry and orange sauce and boil for a further 2–3 minutes, until thick. Remove the pan from the heat and stir in the chilled butter. Set aside.

2 To prepare the salsa: peel the orange, using a small sharp knife, then cut away the flesh into segments. Chop these into small pieces and combine with the remaining ingredients, in a bowl.

3 Heat the oil in a large, non-stick frying pan over a high heat, add the lamb chops and cook for 3–4 minutes on one side, until browned (do this in two batches – cook the first six on one side, remove from the pan, then cook the next batch in the same way). Turn them and return all the chops to the pan. Pour in half the sauce and simmer for 2 minutes, until cooked through and hot. Serve browned-side up with the salsa and extra sauce poured over the chops.

The succulent lamb chops are cooked with a cranberry

Many people prefer the flavour of organic lamb. Like all red meats, it is an excellent source of iron, zinc

and orange sauce. Serving them with the lively orange

and protein. Lamb is slightly fattier than pork or beef, so you may want to trim off some of the fat.

salsa adds a really bright and refreshing touch.

SHEPHERD'S PIE

Serves 4
Preparation 20 mins
Cooking time 1 hour

Calories 527
Fat 25g

Simplicity

1 Heat the oil in a large frying pan, cook the onion and garlic over a medium heat for 5 minutes, until softened. Increase the heat slightly and add the mince. Fry for a further 5 minutes, breaking up any lumps with a wooden spoon, until the meat has browned. Stir in the sauce, together with the parsley, vinegar and seasoning. Simmer, covered, for about 20 minutes, stirring occasionally.

2 Meanwhile, cook the potatoes and carrots in boiling, salted water for 15–20 minutes, until tender. Drain, then mash the potatoes and carrots with the butter and season with black pepper.

3 Preheat the oven to 190°C/375°F/Gas Mark 5. Transfer the mince to a large, shallow, ovenproof dish. Spoon over the mashed potato topping in an even layer and fluff up with a fork. Cook for 35–40 minutes, until the potato is browned, then garnish with extra parsley.

1 tbsp olive oil

1 large onion, chopped

1 garlic clove, crushed

500g (1lb 2oz) minced lamb

390g jar Tomato and basil pasta sauce

2 tbsp chopped fresh parsley, plus extra, to garnish

2 tsp red wine vinegar

Sea salt and freshly ground black pepper

For the topping

675g (1lb 8oz) potatoes, peeled and chopped

225g (8oz) carrots, chopped

50g (2oz) butter

Using an organic pasta sauce for speed, and adding

Unlike most other vegetables, carrots are better for you when cooked, rather than raw, as they can be

carrots to the traditional mashed potato topping, puts

more easily digested. As a result, your body is able to absorb more of the carrots' beta carotene.

a whole new slant on this timeless family favourite.

PAN-FRIED PORK WITH CABBAGE AND APPLES

Simplicity

Serves 4

Preparation 15 mins

Cooking time 30 mins

Calories 462

Fat 25g

15g (½oz) butter

1 tbsp sunflower oil

4 pork loin steaks

1 large red onion, finely chopped

300ml (½ pint) apple juice

1 tbsp Cyder vinegar

Sea salt and freshly ground black pepper

225g (8oz) Savoy cabbage, finely shredded

1 dessert apple, cored and cut into thin strips

1 tsp lemon juice, plus 1 tbsp lemon juice, for the sauce

3 tbsp extra thick cream

1 Heat the butter and 1 teaspoon of oil in a large frying pan. Cook the pork steaks over a high heat for 2 minutes each side, until golden brown. Remove from the pan. Add half the onion to the pan and cook for 2 minutes, until lightly softened and golden. Stir in 200ml (7fl oz) of the apple juice and the Cyder vinegar, and season well. Bring to the boil, then simmer for 5 minutes or until reduced slightly.

2 Heat the remaining oil in a frying pan and cook the remaining onion for about 3 minutes. Add the cabbage, apple, the remaining apple juice, 1 teaspoon of lemon juice and seasoning. Stir-fry for 5 minutes until cooked, but still slightly crisp.

3 Stir the cream into the sauce with 1 tablespoon of lemon juice. Return the pork to the pan, along with any juices and simmer for a further 4 minutes, until heated through. Serve the pork with the cabbage and apple stir-fry on the side.

Based on the classic partnership of pork and apples, this

Pork is naturally leaner than either lamb or beef, but it is still full of vitamins and minerals. Cabbage is

creamy apple sauce is the perfect foil for lean pork loin

an excellent source of vitamin C and eating it twice a week may also help to ward off certain cancers.

steaks. Delicious with really buttery mashed potato.

MEATBALLS WITH SPICY TOMATO SAUCE

Serves 4

Preparation 20 mins

(plus 10 mins chilling)

Cooking time 20 mins

Calories 704

Fat 25g

Simplicity

1 Place the breadcrumbs in a large bowl and combine with the minced beef, bacon, onion, parsley, egg and seasoning and mix well. Shape the mixture into 20 balls and flatten slightly with the palm of your hand. Chill in the fridge for 10 minutes.

2 Heat the oil in a large frying pan and, over a medium to high heat, brown the meatballs on all sides for about 5 minutes (you may need to do this in two batches). Spoon off any excess oil from the frying pan and pour the pasta sauce over the meatballs in the pan. Reduce the heat to medium and simmer gently for 10 minutes, turning the meatballs occasionally, until cooked through.

3 Meanwhile, cook the pasta according to packet instructions, then drain. Serve the meatballs with the pasta and garnish with extra parsley.

50g (2oz) fresh breadcrumbs, made from 2 slices stonebaked white loaf, crusts removed

500g pack minced beef

50g (2oz) bacon, finely chopped (optional)

1 small onion, finely chopped

3 tbsp chopped fresh parsley, plus extra, to garnish

1 medium egg, beaten

Sea salt and freshly ground black pepper

2 tbsp sunflower oil

390g jar Spicy roasted garlic pasta sauce

350g (12oz) dried pasta, such as tagliatelle or penne

Beef is a good source of many B vitamins as well as zinc and iron. Zinc is needed for growth, sexual

An Italian classic – homemade meatballs and tomato

development and a healthy immune system, while iron plays an essential role in helping the body convert

sauce served with pasta. Pile them high and tuck in!

food into energy. Pasta provides a convenient form of energy-providing carbohydrates.

PAN-FRIED STEAKS WITH TOMATO SALSA

Simplicity

Serves 4

Preparation 25 mins
(plus 30 mins marinating)

Cooking time 5 mins

Calories 283

Fat 14g

4 fillet or sirloin steaks, trimmed of any excess fat

4 tbsp red wine

1 tbsp balsamic vinegar

1 garlic clove, crushed

2 tsp sunflower oil

For the salsa

4 tomatoes

½ red onion, finely chopped

2.5cm (1in) piece fresh root ginger, finely chopped (optional)

2 tbsp finely chopped fresh coriander, plus extra, to garnish

1 tbsp extra virgin olive oil

Sea salt and freshly ground black pepper

Sauté potatoes, to serve

1 Place the steaks in a shallow dish. Mix together the red wine, balsamic vinegar and garlic. Pour over the steaks, cover and leave to marinate in the fridge for at least 30 minutes.

2 To make the salsa, place the tomatoes in a bowl, and cover with boiling water for 30 seconds, then drain, peel, deseed and finely chop. Put the flesh in to a bowl with the onion, ginger, if using, coriander, olive oil and seasoning, then mix together. Set aside.

3 Heat the oil in a large, non-stick frying pan, until hot. Add the steaks (reserving the marinade) and cook on a high heat for 2 minutes without moving them. Turn and cook for a further 2 minutes. Add the marinade and cook for 1 minute or until the steaks are cooked to your liking and the sauce has almost evaporated. Remove from the heat and allow the meat to rest for 10 minutes. Serve with the salsa and sauté potatoes, and garnish with extra coriander.

If you have enough time, marinate the steaks overnight

Beef has had a lot of bad press over the last few years, but it is full of valuable nutrients. You can help to

to allow the flavours to develop fully. It'll be better still

reduce your saturated fat intake by choosing leaner cuts of meat, such as trimmed fillet or sirloin steaks.

if you leave the meat to rest for a while after cooking.

CITRUS BREAD AND BUTTER PUDDING

Serves 4

Preparation 45 mins

(including standing time)

Cooking time 40 mins

Calories 654

Fat 44g

Simplicity

1 In a small bowl, mix together the butter, lemon and orange rind and orange juice. Spread the bread with the flavoured butter and cut each slice into four triangles. Sprinkle the raisins over the base of a 1 litre (1¾ pint) greased, shallow, ovenproof dish and arrange the bread on top.

2 Gently heat the cream, and bring just to the boil. In a bowl, whisk the egg yolks with the sugar, until just pale. Pour the cream in and stir well. Pour the mixture over the bread and leave to stand for 20 minutes, to allow the bread to soak up the liquid.

3 Preheat the oven to 200°C/400°F/Gas Mark 6. Place the pudding dish in a large roasting tin. Pour boiling water into the tin to come halfway up the sides of the dish. Bake for 30 minutes, until crisp and golden on top and lightly set. Serve with extra thick cream, if wished, or just on its own.

35g (1¼oz) butter, softened, plus extra, for greasing
Finely grated rind of 1 lemon
Finely grated rind and juice of 1 orange
6 slices white sliced bread, crusts removed
50g (2oz) raisins
250g carton extra thick cream, plus extra, to serve (optional)
4 medium egg yolks
75g (3oz) golden sugar

This traditional nursery pudding is given a fresh twist

White bread, although not thought to be as good as wholemeal bread, is still a good source of fibre and

with the lively, zingy citrus flavours from the oranges

by law it has to be fortified with calcium and B vitamins. Citrus fruits are an excellent source of vitamin C.

and lemons, loved by children and grown-ups.

BRAZIL NUT SHORTBREADS WITH STRAWBERRIES

Simplicity 👨‍🍳 👨‍🍳

Serves 4

Preparation 30 mins

(plus 20 mins chilling)

Cooking time 10–12 mins

Calories 715

Fat 53g

For the shortbread

25g (1oz) brazil nuts

50g (2oz) golden sugar

125g (4oz) plain white flour

75g (3oz) butter, softened

2 medium egg yolks

For the filling

1 tsp grated orange rind, plus extra, to decorate

250g carton extra thick cream

227g punnet strawberries, hulled and sliced

4 tbsp strawberry jam

1 Place the nuts and sugar in a food processor and whizz until fine, add the flour and butter and whizz until it resembles fine breadcrumbs. Add the egg yolks and pulse until the mixture forms a soft dough. (Do not over-process.) Bring the mixture together to form a ball, then wrap in clingfilm and chill for 20 minutes.

2 Preheat the oven to 200°C/400°F/Gas Mark 6. On a lightly floured surface, roll out the dough to 5mm (¼in) thick and stamp out eight 7.5cm (3in) rounds with a biscuit cutter, re-rolling as necessary. Place on a greased baking tray and bake for 10–12 minutes, until lightly golden. Cool on a wire rack.

3 Fold the orange rind into the cream. Place a small amount of cream on a biscuit, top with strawberries, another biscuit, then more cream and strawberries. Warm the jam in a small saucepan, then drizzle it over the top. Decorate with orange rind. Repeat with the remaining biscuits.

Fresh strawberries are sandwiched together with cream,

Strawberries contain more vitamin C than any other berry and a typical portion contains only 28 calories.

between soft melt-in-the-mouth biscuits, and served with

Brazil nuts are rich in selenium, a powerful antioxidant needed for fertility, healthy skin and hair.

a drizzle of strawberry jam – simply delicious.

MANGO OAT CRUNCH

Serves 4

Preparation 15 mins

Cooking time 4–5 mins

Calories 665

Fat 47g

Simplicity

1 To prepare the mangoes, slice the two fatter 'cheeks' of the mangoes from either side of the stone. Cut a criss-cross pattern across the flesh of each piece to divide into small cubes, then push the skin upwards from the centre and carefully slice off the cubes in to a bowl.

2 Melt the butter and sugar in a saucepan and add the porridge oats. Cook over a medium heat for 4–5 minutes, stirring all the time, until the oats are just golden and toasted. Leave to cool slightly.

3 Mix together the soft cheese and crème fraîche in a bowl, add the lemon juice and 2 tablespoons of the honey and combine well. Spoon the oats into individual glasses or serving bowls. Add a layer of the cream mixture, top with the mango, then drizzle over the remaining honey and serve straight away. Alternatively, fold the mango and oats into the cream and serve all combined in glasses or bowls.

2 mangoes
50g (2oz) butter
25g (1oz) golden sugar
125g (4oz) porridge oats
200g carton full fat soft cheese
200g carton crème fraîche
Juice of ½ lemon
4 tbsp clear honey

Juicy mangoes, toasted porridge oats and honey set each other off in this creamy, crunchy dessert. Try using peaches or pineapples, if mangoes are out of season.

The soluble fibre in oats has been found to help lower blood cholesterol and helps to stabilise blood sugar levels. Mangoes are an excellent source of beta carotene, which the body turns into vitamin A.

RICH CHOCOLATE SOUFFLES

Simplicity

Serves 4

Preparation 25 mins

Cooking time 20 mins

Calories 320

Fat 13g

1 tbsp melted butter
100g (3½oz) golden sugar, plus 1 tbsp, for sprinkling
100g pack Green and Black's dark chocolate, broken into pieces
2 tbsp orange juice
2 medium eggs, separated
½ tsp finely grated orange rind
Pinch of salt
Cocoa powder, for dusting (optional)

1 Grease the sides of four individual 125ml (4fl oz) ramekin dishes, or ovenproof soufflé dishes, with the melted butter. Sprinkle the tablespoon of sugar equally between the dishes, dust the sides and shake out any excess. Preheat the oven to 190°C/375°F/ Gas Mark 5 and place a baking sheet in the oven.

2 Heat the chocolate and orange juice in a bowl, over a pan of simmering water, until the chocolate has melted and the mixture is smooth. Remove from the heat and stir in the egg yolks with the orange rind and half the sugar.

3 Whisk the egg whites in a large bowl with a pinch of salt until they form stiff peaks, then slowly whisk in the remaining sugar. Fold a quarter of the egg whites into the chocolate, then fold in the remaining egg whites. Spoon the mixture into the dishes and place in the oven on the hot baking sheet. Cook for 12–14 minutes, until well risen and just set. Dust with cocoa powder, if using, and serve.

These individual, light chocolate soufflés have just a hint

Organic chocolate usually contains much higher levels of cocoa solids than most conventional brands of

of orange. If you think cream is too sinful, try serving

chocolate. As a result it contains more iron, too, and much less sugar and fat.

them with a raspberry sauce (see page 93).

ROASTED PEACHES WITH RASPBERRY SAUCE

Serves 4

Preparation 20 mins

Cooking time 20 mins

Calories 274

Fat 10g

Simplicity

1 To make the sauce, place the raspberries in a food processor with the sugar and orange juice and pulse to combine. Alternatively, crush the raspberries with a fork, add the sugar and orange juice and mix well. Pass the mixture through a sieve to remove any pips and set aside.

2 Preheat the oven to 200°C/400°F/Gas Mark 6. Line an ovenproof dish with baking paper and place the peach halves on top. Dot with the butter, sprinkle with the sugar and drizzle over the honey. Cook for 10 minutes, remove from the oven, sprinkle over the almonds, return to the oven and cook for 10 minutes or until the peaches are soft.

3 To serve, place the peach halves on individual plates and serve with the raspberry sauce.

4 ripe peaches, halved and stoned

25g (1oz) butter

4 tbsp sugar

2 tbsp clear honey

25g (1oz) almonds, halved lengthways

For the sauce

113g punnet raspberries

25g (1oz) golden sugar

4 tbsp orange juice

Ripe peaches are roasted with honey and almonds, until

Almonds are a good source of the antioxidant vitamin E, which is actually found in the oil of the kernel.

soft and almost caramelised. Serve with a dollop of crème

Peaches and raspberries provide another antioxidant – vitamin C – as well as useful amounts of fibre.

fraîche or ice cream to add to their lovely, rich sweetness.

FRUIT SALAD WITH LEMON AND GINGER SYRUP

Simplicity

Serves 4

Preparation 20 mins

(plus 2 hours chilling)

Cooking time 5 mins

Calories 219

Fat 0.4g

3 nectarines, stoned and sliced

227g punnet strawberries, sliced

3 clementines, peeled and segmented

½ cantaloupe or charentais melon, deseeded and sliced

Extra thick cream, to serve (optional)

For the syrup

125g (4oz) golden sugar

Juice of 2 lemons

10cm (4in) piece fresh root ginger, grated

1 To make the syrup, place the sugar in a small, heavy-based saucepan, add the lemon juice and ginger and gently heat, until the sugar is dissolved. Bring to the boil, then simmer for 2 minutes. Strain through a sieve, discarding the ginger.

2 Place the prepared fruits in individual glass bowls or a large glass bowl and pour over the warm syrup. Toss gently and chill for up to 2 hours. Serve with some extra thick cream, if wished.

Ginger and lemon gang up to give this simple dessert an

This fruit salad is packed with all sorts of vitamins and minerals from the delicious fruits. Chewing fresh

unexpected kick. You don't have to stick with these

root ginger is a surprisingly effective remedy for sickness, especially travel and morning sickness.

fruits, just choose your favourites. Serve with cream.

APPLE, PEAR AND BANANA CRUMBLE

Serves 4   **Calories** 560   **Simplicity**

Preparation 20 mins   **Fat** 26g

Cooking time 30–35 mins

1 Preheat the oven to 200°C/400°F/Gas Mark 6. Place the apples and pears in a large, shallow, ovenproof dish, add the apple juice and drizzle over the honey. Lay the bananas on top.

2 Rub the butter into the flour, using your fingertips, until the mixture resembles rough breadcrumbs. Stir in the sugar and spoon this mixture over the bananas.

3 Cook for 30–35 minutes or until the fruit is bubbling and the topping is golden.

2 dessert apples, peeled and sliced

2 ripe pears, peeled, cored and sliced

3 tbsp apple juice

1 tbsp clear honey

2 bananas, sliced

For the topping

125g (4oz) butter, cut into cubes

150g (5oz) plain white flour

75g (3oz) golden sugar

Adding bananas to the fruit filling gives a sweetness to

Bananas are a good source of potassium, which the body needs for muscles to work effectively and is

the crumble, and it goes deliciously toffee-like around the

essential for a healthy nervous system. They are an ideal snack for athletes and growing children.

edges. Serve with cream or crème fraîche.

BABY AND TODDLER FOODS

Making your own homemade baby foods is easy. When you first introduce your baby to solids it doesn't take long to prepare a few simple purées. By doing this, not only will you save money, but you will also know that you are using only the best quality organic ingredients, with no artificial additives or flavourings.

Try either lightly boiling or steaming fruit and vegetables, until cooked, then purée, using a blender or food processor, until smooth. When your child is a little older, between six and nine months, you can adjust the texture of the purée as your baby begins to chew. Giving your baby a selection of tastes early on, will help your child accept new flavours throughout the first habit-forming 12 months of his or her life.

Most foods can be frozen for future meals, so it is a good plan to make more than is needed for one meal. After preparing the purées, allow to cool, then freeze in ice-cube trays until hard. When frozen, knock the cubes out and store in freezer bags labelled with the date and what the purée is. Fruit and vegetable purées can be frozen for up to six months, meat and chicken for up to two months. It's always a good idea to test the temperature of the food before giving it to your baby and serve it just warm.

4-6 MONTHS

When you start weaning your baby onto solids, introduce one food at a time. First foods should be easy to digest; start with baby rice, sweet potato, courgette, parsnip, potato, carrot, apple, banana or pear purées: then, if there is any sort of allergic reaction you will know what caused it.

After the first two months, you can begin combining different foods. At first, purées should be smooth and runny. You can adjust the texture of the purées by adding breast or formula milk, or cooled boiled water to achieve a creamy consistency.

SWEDE WITH PARSNIP AND APPLE

Simplicity

Makes about 6 portions

125g (4oz) swede, chopped
1 medium parsnip, chopped
½ apple, peeled, cored and chopped

1 Place the swede and parsnip in a saucepan and just cover with water. Bring to the boil, then cover and simmer for 10 minutes. Add the apple and simmer for a further 10 minutes, until cooked.

2 Strain the vegetables and apple and reserve the cooking water. Purée and mix to the desired consistency using the reserved water, boiled water, breast or formula milk.

Swede is rich in the antioxidant vitamins A and C and is an ideal weaning food for babies as it is easy

Making your own purées is simple and you can have fun

to digest and combines with other vegetables and fruits very well. Both the parsnip and apple provide

experimenting with different fruits and vegetables.

more vitamin C and give the purée a lovely natural sweetness that babies will love.

CREAM OF PEAR, MELON AND AVOCADO

Simplicity

Makes about 2 portions

125g (4oz) cantaloupe melon, deseeded and chopped
½ pear, peeled, cored and chopped
½ ripe avocado, peeled and stoned

1 Steam the melon and pear together for 5 minutes, then allow to cool slightly. Purée or mash with a fork to a smooth consistency. Mash the avocado and mix in with the melon and pear purée.

2 Serve straight away or the avocado will begin to discolour. However, you can keep it in the fridge, in a sealed container, for up to a day. Not suitable for freezing.

POTATO, CARROT AND CAULIFLOWER

Simplicity

Makes about 4 portions

50g (2oz) potato, peeled and chopped
1 medium carrot, scrubbed and chopped
50g (2oz) cauliflower, cut into small florets

1 Place the potato and carrot in a saucepan and just cover with water. Bring to the boil, cover and simmer for 10 minutes. Add the cauliflower and simmer for a further 10 minutes, until thoroughly cooked. Leave to cool slightly.

2 Strain, reserving the cooking water, then purée and mix to a suitable consistency using the reserved water, boiled water, breast or formula milk.

Most babies take to fruit purées immediately. But to stop Some foods make particularly good bases for purées. Pears are an excellent choice as they rarely trigger **them from developing too much of a sweet tooth, it is** allergic reactions.and the natural starches in cooked potatoes are a great source of energy for infants. **worth encouraging them to eat savoury ones too.**

6–9 MONTHS

Babies can now eat protein foods like cheese, pulses and chicken and it's a good time to introduce plenty of new textures and stronger flavours. Once your baby starts to get teeth and learns to chew, you can introduce coarser textures.

Green beans with tomatoes and peas

Simplicity

Makes about 2–3 portions

50g (2oz) green beans, topped, tailed and chopped
2 tomatoes, skinned, quartered and deseeded
50g (2oz) fresh or frozen peas

1 Steam the beans and tomatoes for about 5 minutes over a medium heat, add the peas and steam for 3 minutes or until cooked. Allow to cool slightly, then purée to a suitable consistency with 1–2 tablespoons of cooled boiled water, breast or formula milk .

CHICKEN WITH SWEETCORN, POTATO AND BROCCOLI

Simplicity

Makes about 6 portions

1 skinless chicken breast, cubed
125g (4oz) potato, peeled and chopped
25g (1oz) broccoli, chopped
50g (2oz) frozen sweetcorn

1 Place the chicken cubes and potato in a medium saucepan and just cover with water, bring to the boil, cover and simmer for 20 minutes. Add the broccoli and sweetcorn and simmer for a further 5 minutes. Allow to cool slightly.

2 Strain, reserving the cooking water, purée and mix to a suitable consistency using the reserved water, cooled boiled water, or breast or formula milk.

PEACH AND BANANA RICE PUDDING

Simplicity

Makes about 2–3 portions

25g (1oz) white fragrant rice
150ml (¼ pint) apple juice
1 peach, skinned, stoned and chopped
½ ripe banana, chopped

1 Place the rice in a medium saucepan with the apple juice. Bring to the boil, cover and simmer for 20 minutes or until the rice is cooked. Allow to cool slightly.

2 Strain the rice, reserving the apple juice, and purée together with the peach and banana. Mix with a fork, to a suitable consistency using the apple juice. Cover and keep in the fridge and use as required. Not suitable for freezing.

Now is the time to get your baby used to different flavours and textures. Each meal should combine

Experiment with different foods. Try sweet potato in the

a good balance of the four food groups – dairy, fruit and vegetables, protein and carbohydrates.

chicken purée and mango works well in the rice pudding.

Chicken is a good choice for babies of this age as it is high in protein, vitamin B12 and iron.

9-12 MONTHS

At this stage you can start to vary the diet you give your baby a little more. Use herbs and garlic to introduce some stronger flavours and try out different consistencies; you no longer need to purée everything.

Apple breakfast yogurt

Simplicity

Makes about 3–4 portions

50g (2oz) porridge oats
4 tbsp apple juice
1 apple, peeled, cored and grated
1 peach, peeled, stoned and finely chopped
1 kiwi, peeled, cored and finely chopped
50g (2oz) natural yogurt

1 In a small bowl, mix together the porridge oats and apple juice. Cover and refrigerate overnight. Mix the fruit into the oats, stir in the yogurt and serve.

CHICKEN WITH TOMATO AND COURGETTE

Simplicity

Makes about 2 portions

1 tbsp olive or sunflower oil
¼ onion, finely chopped
1 skinless chicken breast, finely chopped
1 medium courgette, finely chopped
1 tbsp apple juice
1 tomato, skinned, deseeded and chopped
1 tbsp fresh basil, finely chopped

1 Heat the oil in a small saucepan over a medium heat and cook the onion for 2 minutes, then add the chicken and cook for a further 3 minutes. Add the courgette and apple juice, cover and simmer for a further 8 minutes.

2 Stir in the tomatoes and basil and cook for a further 2 minutes or until the vegetables are tender and the chicken is cooked through. Chop or purée to the desired consistency.

Now is the time to build the foundations of a healthy

A good breakfast is vitally important. Oats provide valuable amounts of soluble fibre and are high in

balanced diet. Developing good habits early on is the best

complex carbohydrates which release energy gradually throughout the morning.

way to ensure children don't become fussy eaters later.

12 MONTHS PLUS

Toddlers can now eat more or less the same foods that adults are eating. In fact, as their taste buds develop, they will enjoy eating a surprising range of foods and will even take to quite strong flavours. Introducing them to as wide a variety of foods and tastes as possible at this age is the best way to ensure that they grow up liking most things and don't end up becoming fussy eaters.

Mealtimes should be fun, so try to eat as a family as often as you can, or at least try to eat something with your children, to make the whole eating process an enjoyable social occasion. Your children will learn how to eat by example and enjoy their meals more.

At 12 months, you can give them whole cow's milk. Growing toddlers and children require dietary fat and should not be given low-fat products or skimmed milk.

VEGETABLE CHEESY PASTA

Serves 6

Preparation 10 mins

Cooking time 15 mins

Calories 408

Fat 16g

Simplicity

1 Cook the pasta according to packet instructions. When it is almost cooked, add the frozen mixed vegetables and cook for 3 minutes, until the pasta is tender and the vegetables have softened. Drain and return to the pan.

2 Meanwhile, melt the butter in a saucepan over a low heat. Add the flour and cook for 1–2 minutes, stirring. Remove from the heat and gradually add the milk, stirring until smooth. Return to the heat and bring to the boil. Simmer, uncovered, for 5 minutes, until thickened. Add the cheese and stir until melted. Toss the pasta and vegetables in the sauce and cool a little before serving.

225g (8oz) dried pasta, such as gemelli or other favourite shape

175g (6oz) frozen mixed vegetables

25g (1oz) butter

25g (1oz) plain white flour

300ml (½ pint) full fat milk

75g (3oz) Cheddar cheese, grated

This simple pasta dish can be whipped up in no time at

The cheese and milk in this recipe provide calcium, which toddlers need for healthy bones and teeth. This

all and is perfect for active children who need plenty

dish also supplies other nutrients – iron, potassium, vitamins C and E and a range of B vitamins.

of calories and carbohydrates to renew their energy!

SPANISH OMELETTE WITH PEAS AND SWEETCORN

Simplicity

Serves 4

Preparation 10 mins

Cooking 18 mins

Calories 182

Fat 12g

2 tbsp olive oil
2 small potatoes, peeled and cut into 1cm (½in) cubes
¼ onion, finely chopped
½ red pepper, deseeded and finely chopped
25g (1oz) frozen peas
25g (1oz) frozen sweetcorn
4 eggs

1 Heat the oil in a 23cm (9in), non-stick frying pan with a heatproof handle. Fry the potatoes and onion for 5 minutes, until softened and golden.

2 Add the pepper, peas and sweetcorn and cook for a further 4 minutes, stirring occasionally. Beat the eggs together and pour this mixture into the pan, over the vegetables. Cook over a medium heat for about 6 minutes or until just set.

3 Preheat the grill to medium. Place the pan under the grill and cook for 2–3 minutes, until the top is golden brown and the omelette is cooked through.

Colour is very important in the presentation of food

Eggs are a great food for toddlers – they are easy to eat and they're packed with vitamins and minerals,

when getting children to try new things; contrasting

such as iron, needed for healthy growth, and phosphorus, which helps the absorption of other nutrients.

colours can help make the meal look more appetising.

CHICKEN AND ONION BURGERS WITH APPLE

Cooking 15 mins

Calories 107

Fat 3g

Serves 4

Preparation 30 mins
(including chilling time)

Simplicity

1 Place the minced chicken in a mixing bowl with the spring onion, breadcrumbs, apple and tomato ketchup. Mix all the ingredients together well, then, using your hands, shape into four 9cm (3½in) flat patties. Cover and chill for 20 minutes.

2 Preheat the grill to high. Grease a baking sheet. Place the patties on the baking sheet and grill for 5–6 minutes, then turn them over and grill for a further 5–6 minutes or until the chicken burgers are cooked through and lightly golden.

3 Serve with buns or rolls and tomato ketchup on the side, if wished.

2 skinless chicken breasts, minced in a food processor

1 spring onion, finely chopped

2 tbsp fresh breadcrumbs, made from 1 slice stonebaked white loaf, crusts removed

1 eating apple, peeled, cored and grated

2 tsp tomato ketchup, plus extra, to serve (optional)

Oil, for greasing

Chicken tends to be popular with babies, as the flavour

Poultry is a good source of protein and minerals. Chicken also supplies valuable amounts of most of the

isn't too strong. It's also a very adaptable food and can be

B vitamins. Tomato ketchup is much healthier than most other sauces – so let them get stuck in...

incorporated into many different dishes.

INDEX

USEFUL ADDRESSES AND NUMBERS:

Soil Association
Bristol House, 40–56 Victoria Street, Bristol, BS1 6BY.
Tel: 0117 929 0661.
Website: www.soilassociation.org

Tesco helpline: 0800 505 555
(for advice and information on Tesco goods and services).